C000111410

SCHUMANN

ETUDES EN FORME DE VARIATIONS
("Symphonic Etudes")

**OPUS 13
FOR THE PIANO**

EDITED BY MAURICE HINSON

AN ALFRED MASTERWORK EDITION

Alfred Music Publishing Co., Inc.
P.O. Box 10003
Van Nuys, CA 91410-0003
alfred.com

Book Alone:
ISBN-10: 0-7390-8191-8
ISBN-13: 978-0-7390-8191-4
Book & CD:
ISBN-10: 0-7390-7764-3
ISBN-13: 978-0-7390-7764-1

*Cover art: Golden Autumn, 1895
by Isaac Levitan (1860–1900)
Tretyakov Gallery, Moscow, Russia
Scala/Art Resource, New York*

ROBERT SCHUMANN
Etudes en forme de Variations ("Symphonic Etudes"), Op. 13

Maurice Hinson, Editor

This edition is dedicated to
Claudette Sorel
with admiration and
appreciation.

Maurice Hinson

Example 1. *1835 manuscript of the first page showing Schumann's thoughts on the development of the title*

Background

Like many of Schumann's extended works, the *Etudes en forme de Variations* ("Symphonic Etudes") are the product of a lengthy and complicated evolution. The theme of great elegiac beauty is from a set of variations by Baron Ignaz von Fricken. Schumann fell violently in love with von Fricken's daughter Ernestine while they both were students of Friedrich Wieck. Von Fricken sent the variations to Schumann for criticism in 1834. Schumann replied at length, critical of much of the music but polite and encouraging. He was, after all, addressing the man he regarded as his future father-in-law.

> I am happy to have your composition as a point of contact. Whether it will spin into a longer thread, holding us together at a distance, I don't know, but that is my wish. … You already realize without my having to say it that I am ardently interested in your inestimable Ernestine as an artist. How eagerly I want her to enjoy every step of progress we might make.[1]

A visit was arranged in Leipzig so that Schumann and the baron could meet. The baron presented himself to Schumann as a humble amateur, ingratiatingly playing the flute and seeking more advice about his set of variations. Later in 1834, Schumann wrote to von Fricken saying, "I actually have been writing variations on your theme, and am going to call them 'Pathetic,' still if there is anything pathetic about them I have endeavored to portray it in different colors."[2] In 1835 he termed the manuscript *Variations pathétiques* and later removed variations he considered too sad or sentimental. Five have been published posthumously. See pages 48 to 59. In Example 1 (1835 manuscript), the title *Variations*

pathétiques (which would suggest grief) is crossed out.

Schumann later projected a set of 12 etudes. These were probably inspired by the daring, virtuosic and sophisticated Chopin etudes, published in 1833. This version was to have had the title *Zwölf* [12] *Davidsbündler Etüden*. Throughout the next three years the etude character of this composition gave way to the variation format. A manuscript from this period entitled *Tema, quasi marcia funebre* (see Example 2 on page 4) contains some of the material for the present work.

The words of its heading are revealing: *Tema*, the musical substance containing the essential nature of the work; *quasi*, only the suggestion of resemblance (and typical of Schumann's interpretative feeling); *marcia funebre*, the mood at a moment in life caused by a death. In preparation for the 1837 publication, Schumann entitled the work, *Etüden im Orchestercharakter für Pianoforte von Florestan und Eusebius*. However, the publisher Haslinger wanted the work to be issued under Schumann's name (dropping "von Florestan und Eusebius"), and so it appeared with the title *XII Etudes Symphoniques pour le Pianoforte*. The variations were dedicated to the young English composer William Sterndale Bennett (1816–1875), whose work Schumann championed. See Example 3 on page 5.

In 1852 Schumann again reworked the composition. He eliminated the third and ninth numbers, revised the Finale and devised the work's final title, *Etudes en forme de Variations*. It is now more commonly known by its subtitle "Symphonic Etudes." See Example 4 on page 5.

Schumann's decision for this final title was influenced partially by the Mendelssohn title *Variations sérieuses* (1841). As Schumann felt that the term *variation* was inappropriate for Etude III (Vivace) and Etude IX (Presto possible), he omitted Etudes III and IX but retained the term *etude*, incorporating it into the final title. After Schumann's death, the work was published yet again in 1862, with Etudes III and IX reinstated. This is the edition now most commonly used. Finally, in 1893, the five variations that Schumann rejected from his earlier editions were printed by Brahms in the *Supplementary Volume of Schumann's Complete Works*. They are included in the present edition as an appendix (pages 48 to 59). A sixth variation remains unpublished.

---

1 Schumann, *Jugendbriefe*, 251–55.
2 Program notes, 1.

Example 2. *Theme, Op. 13*

About This Edition

This edition is based on Schumann's 1852 revised edition, published by J. Schuberth, Hamburg, plate number 1525. Also consulted for textural differences was the complete edition, edited by Clara Schumann and Johannes Brahms, Leipzig, 1881–93.

Parenthetical material is editorial. Fingerings in italics are Schumann's, others are editorial. All pedal and metronomic indications are Schumann's. More or less pedal than indicated may be used.

I am grateful to the staff of the Bibliothèque de Château Mariemont, Le Morlanwelz, Belgium, for providing microfilm material of the January 18, 1835 manuscript.

Sources Consulted in the Preparation of This Edition

I wish to thank the authors and editors of the works quoted in this collection:

Jost, Mack. *Practice, Interpretation, Performance.* West Melbourne, Australia: Jenkins Buxton Printers, 1984.

Maxwell, Carolyn, and William DeVan, eds. *Schumann Solo Piano Literature.* Boulder, CO: Maxwell Music Evaluation Books, 1984.

Ostwald, Peter. *Schumann: The Inner Voices of a Musical Genius.* Boston: Northeastern University Press, 1985.

Program notes, *Schumann: Piano Music.* Vox Records, SVBX5468.

Schumann, Robert. *Jugendbriefe.* 2d ed.; edited by Clara Schumann. Leipzig: Breitkopf & Härtel, 1886. English trans., May Herbert, 1888. *Early Letters of Robert Schumann.* London: G. Bell & Sons.

About the Music

Etudes en forme de Variations ("Symphonic Etudes") is one of the most astonishing musical accomplishments of the 19th century. A gigantic work, it demonstrates the piano's unique expressive potential. Schumann proved that without an orchestra, the piano can reproduce an orchestral polyphony and a vast range of unprecedented tonal effects. The potentially orchestral character of piano sonorities recalls Beethoven. This work is as significant for Schumann as were the *Goldberg Variations* for Bach, or the *Diabelli Variations* for Beethoven.

The set consists of a theme, seven variations, two etudes and a lengthy Finale. Each (except the Finale) is a binary form, but any potential monotony is deftly circumvented. Schumann manipulated the variation form with an unsurpassed mastery and originality. His genius for the romantic miniature is synthesized through his use of extended dramatic structure.

Schumann's interest in the etude and variation genres achieves an astonishing consummation in this work. He reveals the etude character of the piece in a challenging and marvelously inventive pianism, while employing a variation

Example 3. *First page of the first edition of Op. 13, 1837, with the title* XII Etudes Symphoniques pour le Pianoforte. *Tobias Haslinger (Wien), 1837*

form that is a miracle of structured clarity. Here is some of Schumann's most glittering keyboard writing. The work contains pianistically difficult textures and wild jumps that challenge pianists, no matter how big their technique. Each movement is a study in an aspect of technique such as chords, pedaling or leaps. At the same time, it remains connected (through melodic or harmonic implications) with the Baron's theme. The exceptions are Etudes III and IX and the Finale, which are not derived from the theme. The orchestral tone is immediately apparent, with drumbeats in Variation I, horns and trombones in Variation II. Etude II features violinlike arpeggios over a broad, cellolike theme. Delicate Mendelssohnian flutes and piccolos are heard in Etude IX; a languor reminiscent of Chopin is evident in Variation IX.

These variations are among the greatest of the Romantic era. Without the example of this monumental work, familiar pieces such as the *Variations on a Theme by Handel*, Op. 24, and the *Paganini Variations*, Op. 35, by Brahms, would be unimaginable. Schumann's emotional contrasts are immensely powerful and sometimes extremely abrupt. Often, the variation form is merely a vehicle for virtuosic display. Yet, Schumann brings to the form a seriousness and high purpose which lend a somberness to even the most bravura sections.

The numbering system can be somewhat confusing, as some of the 12 pieces bear the same numbers, as etudes and as variations.

Theme 12

A grave, tragic quality permeates this organlike theme and indicates the general character of the ensuing variations. It should be played adagio, not andante, but Schumann's metronome mark corrects this misnomer. Its simple strophic structure of four regular phrases is ingenious, both harmonically and melodically. Bring out the theme in the octaves in measure 1 and sound the bass whole notes distinctly throughout the measure. Spread the arpeggiated chords (measures 2–4) on the beat and not before, so that all notes will be caught by the pedal. Use the same approach in measures 6–7 and 14–15, if you have to arpeggiate the left-hand 10ths. The sustained trill with melody in the same hand (measures 10–12) conveys the effect of a gentle murmur. In measure 10, play the grace note lightly as a very slight anticipation. Give plenty of resonance to the climax of measure 14. Hold the fermata in this measure at least five quarter beats.

Technical problems include widely spaced arpeggiated chords, tonal control needed for rhythmic and textural subtlety, and fifth-finger melody in chordal structures.

Example 4. *Revised title, Op. 13. Schuberth & Co. (Hamburg, Leipzig, New York), 1852*

This rough-hewn variation reflects Schumann's dual personality: the fiery Florestan and the poetic Eusebius. These two companions, who had been in Schumann's mind since 1831, spoke to him in his imagination, suggested ideas for musical and literary works, and provided support during times of emotional stress. A spectral march emerges and winds its way through ascending registers. Measures 1–4 must be dry and crisp with a rhythmic spring. Maintain staccato touch whenever the 32d note occurs. Beat 4 of measure 4 should be rather lyrical. Maintain tautness and precision in the bass of measure 7; a loose triplet rhythm is unacceptable. Breathe at the end of measure 8. After the sustained legato expansiveness of measures 10–12 resume a light springy touch. This variation calls for a skillful voicing technique. In light of the limited dynamic range, a focused, well-controlled tone is particularly important.

Technical challenges include legato melody with staccato accompaniment, legato chordal passages, wide stretches and a restricted dynamic range requiring subtle tonal control in the lower register.

A bravura, swaggering quality permeates this variation. In measures 1–4, the first phrase of the theme is contained in the left hand. For better emphasis, some pianists play each note of the left-hand theme with the side of the thumb. Schumann's metronomic indication allows enough time to do this. The last three beats of measure 4 may be helpfully redistributed as follows:

Example 5

Variation II, measure 4, the last three beats

Breathe a little before beginning measure 5. Practice the left hand separately in measures 10–12 until you can shape it beautifully. In measure 13, begin the crescendo very quietly to enhance its effectiveness. The final measure (18) must crescendo to the sforzando. Throughout this haunting variation a passionately lyrical melody is displayed against a brooding repeated-chord background. With careful voicing, both right-hand melody and left-hand theme may be disentangled from the relentless accompaniment figures.

Other technical problems include fast register changes, legato octaves and sudden dynamic changes.

Etude III...17

This etude bears only a tenuous relationship to the theme. It should be practiced legato until it can be played at full speed. The most helpful practice rhythms are:

and the reverse:

Let the arm sweep through the almost two octaves while the fingers play the notes almost accidentally on the way. Practice the left hand separately to artistically shape the beautiful melody. Use little or no pedal in measures 7 and 19 where the theme descends so far in the bass clef. In measure 14, play the first left-hand C-sharp on the beat and the rest of the chord (F-sharp and B) on the second eighth beat. This will avoid interrupting the melody. Avoid any ritard at the end. The supreme challenge of this demanding etude is that it must convey the impression of effortless ease and nonchalance.

Fast staccato and legato figuration with sudden register shifts, leaps, wide stretches and maintaining complete hand independence are among the technical problems.

Variation III...19

This variation is undeniably extroverted. An ingenious canon unfolds at the octave where the rhythmically simplified theme is presented in blocked chords. Use arm weight and keep the hands close to the keys. Carefully observe the sforzandos; they provide an arresting quality and highlight the canon at the octave construction. In measures 6–8, keep the rhythm taut and think of the 16ths as grace notes.

Technical problems include widely spaced blocked chords, hand independence and left-hand grace notes. Proceed immediately to Variation IV.

Variation IV...20

This scherzolike variation contains canonic imitation and is pervaded by a single rhythmic figure. Use a very light, close-to-the-keys, forearm stroke. Maintain a taut and sharply defined rhythm. Do not blur its crisp outlines by overpedaling. Move ahead slightly measures 7 and 15. Carefully observe the sforzandos in the second half; they provide an explosive quality that contrasts with the light, crisp texture of the first half.

The technical demands are considerable. Especially troublesome is the close proximity of the hands at the beginning. Other technical challenges include fast staccato octaves, leaps and hand independence.

Variation V...22

A mood of intense agitation is created by a constant syncopated displacement of the theme. Do not allow the accented left-hand upbeat to sound like a downbeat. This precipitous variation must sound exciting but not excited. This means the pianist must maintain full control in the nearly ceaseless swirl of notes. Only in measures 8 and 17 does this relent slightly. Pedal each beat to avoid an overly "busy" sound. Play the left-hand low A rather deliberately in measure 6 for greater accuracy. Use lateral, close movement for the breathtaking left-hand leaps. The forearm does most of the work with the upper arm relatively still.

Other technical problems include two-note slurs, legato melody in the fifth finger and chordal texture against staccato accompaniment.

Variation VI...24

This variation is based on the lower mordent figure persistent throughout the piece. The theme can be emphasized slightly by subordinating the second and third 16th note of each group. These should be considered ornamental. In measures 25–30, play the thundering left-hand octaves with an undulating wrist and forearm. Only the first octave of each group of four is important. Subtle dynamics will avoid the monotony caused by a strictly forte (*sempre brillante*) presentation.

Technical problems include rapid repeated chords, three-note slurs, wide leaps, legato octaves and dynamic control.

Variation VII 26

There is an embroidered quality to this magical variation. It can generally be played gracefully, but a sense of rhythmic propulsion is essential. Mentally listen to the theme while playing. Clearly distinguish between the 64th notes and the 32d-note triplets. Initially count 16th-note microbeats to hear the difference. Measures 7–9 need a warmer, gentler tone quality after the great heroic leaps of measures 1–6. Do not play the trill in measure 9 too loud. The bass octaves in measures 15–17 need an organlike quality; the indication *tenuto per il pedale* (hold the pedal) refers to the dotted half notes. The pedal is released at the harmonic change on the fourth beat.

Other technical problems include complex rhythms, trills and hand independence.

This effervescent Mendelssohn-like scherzo is essentially an independent work. It bears no resemblance to the theme, and although written in 3/16, is grouped rhythmically into units of four measures. This creates the impression of triplets in quadruple time. All four voices must therefore be equally clear in measures 1–8. Practice bringing out the voices: first alto, then tenor and then bass. Aim for a very light, fast wrist action. Use various rhythms:

for measures 34–41. In measures 18 and 22, strongly strike each dotted-eighth G-sharp and E. Begin measures 34 and 38 decisively, but do not play the succeeding measures at the same fortissimo level. It is easier to play the mordents in measures 47 and 55 with the right hand; the tied chord is sustained by the pedal. This will not produce a muddy sonority when played at the *Presto possibile* tempo. Measures 58–60 and 62–64 contain arpeggiated right-hand chords. Combine these with arpeggiated left-hand chords. Play both very fast, emphasizing in both hands those notes played by the thumb. Use no pedal in measure 74 to the end. The final three chords should be very lightly scherzando.

Leaps and full, fast staccato chords are the greatest technical problems.

This variation is full of irrepressible energy. Keep the left hand almost staccato. Do not speed up; the intrinsic beauty of the left-hand figuration must be maintained. Think of the fourth 16th-note chord of the right hand as belonging to the next chord. Maintain a driving, vital rhythm and breathe at the double bar (measures 8 and 16). Treat measures 11–12 lyrically with a slight broadening before returning to the driving rhythm at measure 13. Emphasize strongly the bass line of measures 15–16. Use pedal sparingly.

Technical problems include fast staccato scalar passages, sudden dynamic changes, staccato chordal passages and legato octaves.

This is the most truly lyrical of the variations. It is also the most impressionistic, in which a subtle left-hand accompaniment highlights variants of the right-hand theme. Use the following approach for the quintuplet eighth notes against sixteen 32ds: First, aim for a beautifully even quintuplet. Next, add the skeleton of the left hand's rhythmic framework (measure 2)—the first G-sharp and the C-double-sharp that occurs on beat 4. It is important to play the C-double-sharp exactly halfway between the third and fourth notes of the quintuplet. After this procedure is perfected, it is easier to fit in the rest of the shimmering 32ds. Aim for a gorgeous tone in the theme; use close fingers and arm weight. Practice each voice alone in the right-hand duet (measure 6 to the end). Shape each voice as beautifully as possible, then combine them. Measures 15–21 contain one of Schumann's most beautiful epilogues, full of wistfulness and regret. Long, shallow pedaling will help avoid heavy textures. It will also enhance the effects of mistiness, shimmer and fading away.

Technical problems include cross-rhythms, fast chordal accompaniment, murmuring figuration, long melodic lines, wide stretches and two independent voices in the same hand.

The heroic Finale, a pseudomarch, is written in the tonic major key, enharmonically respelled as D-flat. It should be a little deliberate at the beginning: pedal the first-beat chord and do not rush off of it. All of the staccato chords should be dry and biting. The movement was intended as an elaborate compliment to composer William Sterndale Bennett, to whom the variations were dedicated. Bennett informed Schumann that he played it successfully in England.

> Schumann, still unmarried in 1837 when he published his "Symphonic Etudes," had become infatuated with another attractive young man, the British composer William Sterndale Bennett (1816–1875). By ending his first major composition with a march based on "Proud England Rejoice," he may have been trying both to drum out the humiliation of his broken engagement to Ernestine and to celebrate this new friendship.[3]

The main theme comes from the phrase "Proud England, Rejoice," in Heinrich Marschner's (1795–1861) opera *Der templer und die Jüdin*. The opera is based on Sir Walter Scott's *Ivanhoe*. The tune is sung to words about the hero Richard the Lionhearted, pride of England.

Example 6

Finale, measure 1

Juxtaposed against this music is material derived from the original variation theme. The Finale uses a modified sonata-rondo form of large scope and dramatic impact. A single rhythmic figure permeates the movement. Although the dotted rhythms verge on the obsessive, with skillful presentation they create enormous impetus and provide a vital unifying force.

The technical demands are great, especially in measure 15, which presents a nearly impossible problem for smaller hands. Practice the left hand of this measure in varied ways, including the following:

Example 7

Finale, measure 15

In the choralelike section (measures 18–76), keep a strict rhythm. In general, play very lightly. This movement should gradually intensify in a series of waves to the culminating point of each major climax. The last great climax occurs at the beginning of the coda. Here, at the pickup to measure 177, it moves into B-flat major. At this point, the Finale has the biggest

---

3 Ostwald, 112n.

tone of all.

The material is repeated twice, though sections of it are in different keys. A third statement of the opening theme is well under way when the coda intervenes and brings the work to a triumphal close. Bringing each section to precisely the same dynamic level may prompt the listener to think, "Here we go again!" Therefore, strive for dynamic variation. Equally important are Schumann's pedal indications. Their observance is crucial for the proper range of color and sonority. Measures 187–194 require a stringendo which should broaden in the final three measures, thus concluding the work with a cry of victorious triumph.

Among the technical problems are widely spaced blocked chords with skips, sudden dynamic changes, repeated notes, wide dynamic range and textural changes. In general, the piece demands good physical endurance.

Schumann did not live to see the "Symphonic Etudes" become a permanent part of the repertoire. Today it is one of a trio of his most popular piano works (the other two are *Carnaval*, Op. 9, and the C major *Fantasie*, Op. 17) and a regular concert hall visitor.

APPENDIX OF FIVE SUPPLEMENTARY VARIATIONS TO THE "SYMPHONIC ETUDES"

Schumann ejected these variations from the initial publication of the "Symphonic Etudes." Though completed in 1837, they were not made available until 1893. That year, Brahms included them in the complete edition of *Robert Schumann: Werke*, published by Breitkopf & Härtel. Six unpublished variations were found among Schumann's sketches, but Brahms chose to release only five. Clara was against their publication because she did not feel they were up to the standard of the published work. Because the original manuscript lacked virtually all tempo, dynamic, and expressive indications, Brahms supplied appropriate and effective editorial suggestions. With the exception of the fourth supplementary variation, which was intended to precede the Finale, Schumann's projected ordering of these movements is unknown. Variations I, IV and V are not orchestral in concept. Because of their great beauty, it has become common to interpolate these bravura miniatures into performances of the "Symphonic Etudes." However, this practice is completely contrary to Schumann's intentions. In a work so meticulously organized, disruption of the structural unity can be disastrous. Yet some pianists feel that excluding the supplementary variations deprives the listener of the fullness of Schumann's treatment. Therefore, they are included for the sake of completeness. They may also be played as an independent group; they are far too beautiful to ignore.

Variation I 48

In this delicate harmonic painting the theme is generally presented by the left hand. Meanwhile, the right hand exhibits a flurry of increasingly difficult 32d notes. The second half (measure 9) opens with the theme in the right hand; the left hand provides the swirling accompanimental pattern. By measure 13 the original distribution is restored. Of the supplementary variations, this attractive work most closely resembles a technical exercise.

Important technical considerations include fast accompanimental figuration with wide stretches, as well as octaves and finger facility prompted by wide or awkward leaps, frequent hand position changes and crescendos.

Variation II 50

The opening four measures of this unusual episodic variation contain two pairs of phrases based on question–answer relationships. In both pairs the interrogative phrase exploits the upper registers, while the reply utilizes the bass with a lengthy hand-crossing passage. The left hand confronts widely spaced chords that may challenge the pianist with small hands. Measures 1–4 are unrelated to the theme, but the theme is prominent in the tempestuous tremolo passage (measures 5–8) that immediately follows. This section (measures 5–8) is markedly virtuosic, yet a shimmering veil of sound is preferable to individual clarity of notes.

This demanding variation is fraught with awkward hand-crossings and chordal grace notes. Other technical problems include tremolos; fast, arpeggiated broken chords; long melodic line in legato octaves; scales; hand-crossings and chordal grace notes.

Variation III 54

This variation has a dialogue-duet character. A suggestion of appoggiaturas slightly shade the melodic chordal figure in the triplet accompaniment. An unusual **A B B** form (**A** = measures 1–8; **B** = 9–16; **B** = 17–24) adds variety to this imposing variation. The double-stemmed notes in the bass mark the theme and central melodies: use a penetrating, carefully voiced approach. Considerable rhythmic momentum is generated through constantly flowing triplets. Schumann provided no character or metronome indications for this variation. Therefore, it should not be played fast and energetically (as is often done today) but rather deliberate, with subtle rubato, like a dialogue-duet. Its solidity and grandeur should not degenerate into bombast.

Technical problems include wide leaps, cross rhythms, heavily textured right-hand accompaniment and a wide dynamic range.

Variation IV 56

Schumann originally conceived this evocative variation as a prelude to the Finale. A wistful and elegantly melancholy waltz, it is the only movement among those intended for the "Symphonic Etudes" in triple meter. It is strongly suggestive of a Chopin mazurka. A simple format of melody and accompaniment is used throughout this exquisite piece. Its texture is enlivened by grace notes and 16th-note arabesques. Use a wide range of expressive nuance and touch. Protracted pedaling will strengthen the climactic moments.

Technical problems include syncopation, leaps and long, single-note melodic lines.

Variation V 58

This extraordinary variation, with its wide keyboard spacing and long floating lines, was first planned as an independent movement. It was later designated as the middle section of Etude X in the 1837 (first) edition. It saliently displays many typical Schumann mannerisms. Among these are the use of continuous syncopation through accent displacement, plus a perpetual motion figuration. Composed in binary form, this variation exploits the upper registers that are common in Schumann's works. The high register is responsible for the work's fleeting charm. The final plagal cadence (measure 16) is especially effective, and calls for a warm, richly sonorous tone.

Technical problems include broken-chord figurations spanning large intervals, a syncopated melodic line, melody within a chordal figuration and wide stretches.

The "Symphonic Etudes" magnificently display Schumann's creative genius and pianistic resources. This highly effective masterpiece exerted great influence on Brahms, especially his variation technique, and on future composers.

Etudes en forme de Variations
("*Symphonic Etudes*")
Theme

(a) The 1837 and 1852 editions used small print for the accompaniment to the theme (see Examples 3 and 4, pg. 5). The 1837 edition contained the following note: "The notes of the melody are composed by an amateur."

(b) Schumann's pedal marks (Pedal, Ped., 🎵) mean the damper (right) pedal should be used at the performer's discretion as opposed to being held down until the release sign (∗); sometimes there is no release sign.

Variation I

Variation II

Etude III ⓐ

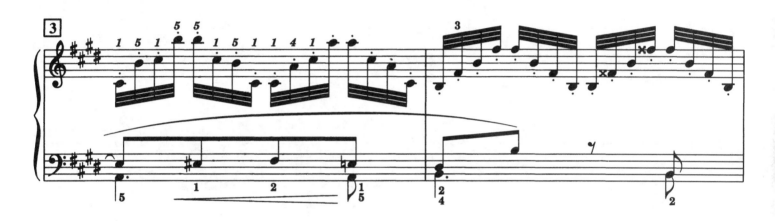

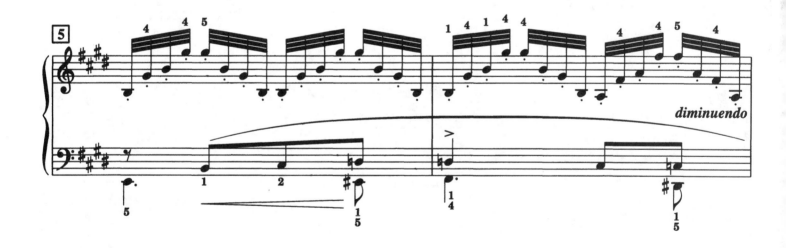

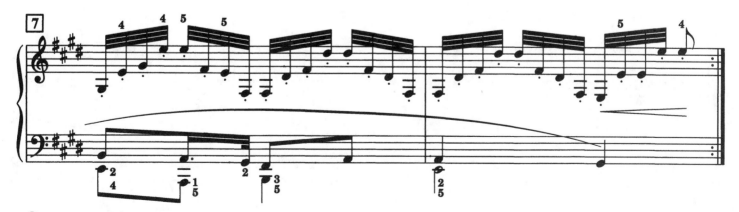

ⓐ Only in the 1852 version.

Variation III

Variation IV

Variation V

Variation VI

Variation VII

28

Etude IX ⓐ

Presto possibile ♪. = 116

senza Pedale

ⓐ Only in the 1852 version.

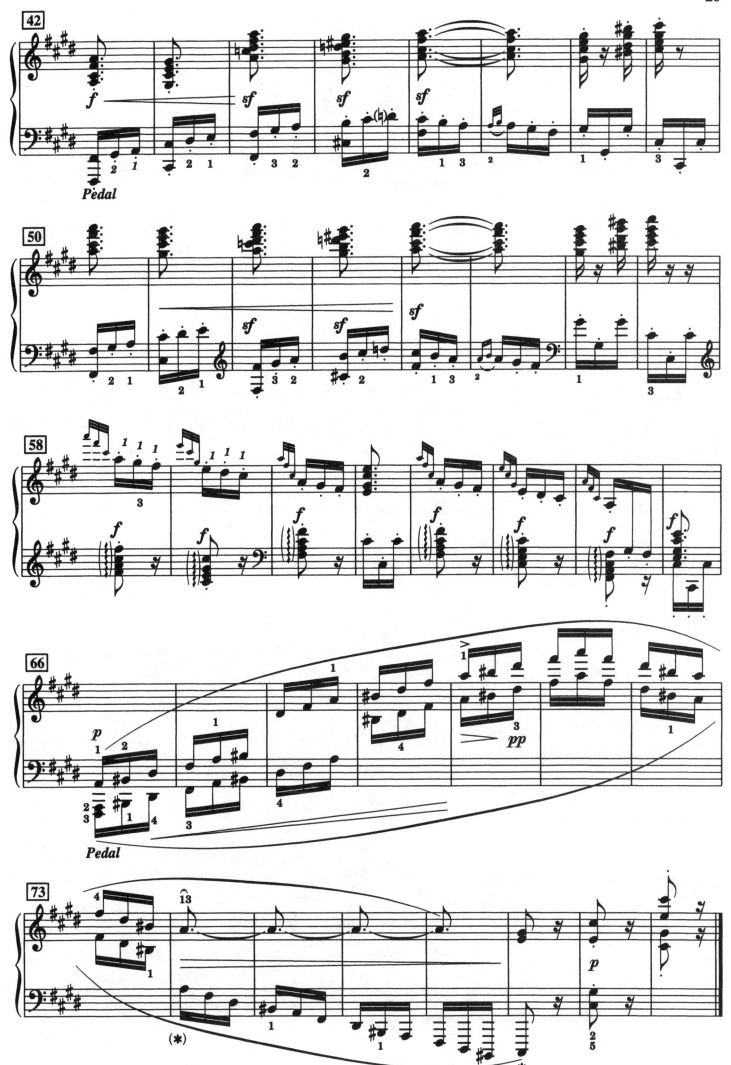

Variation VIII

Variation IX

(a) Measure 1 is not included in the 1852 edition; here added from the 1837 edition.

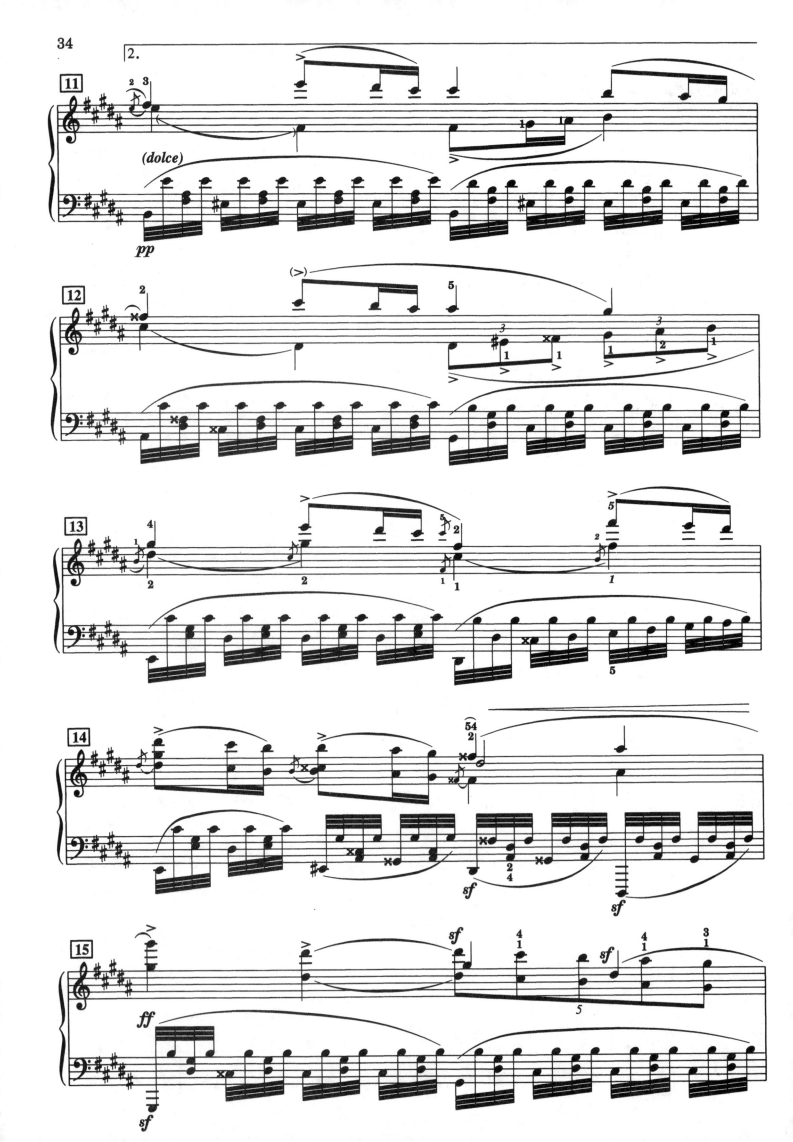

poco a poco morendo

Finale

43

Pedal

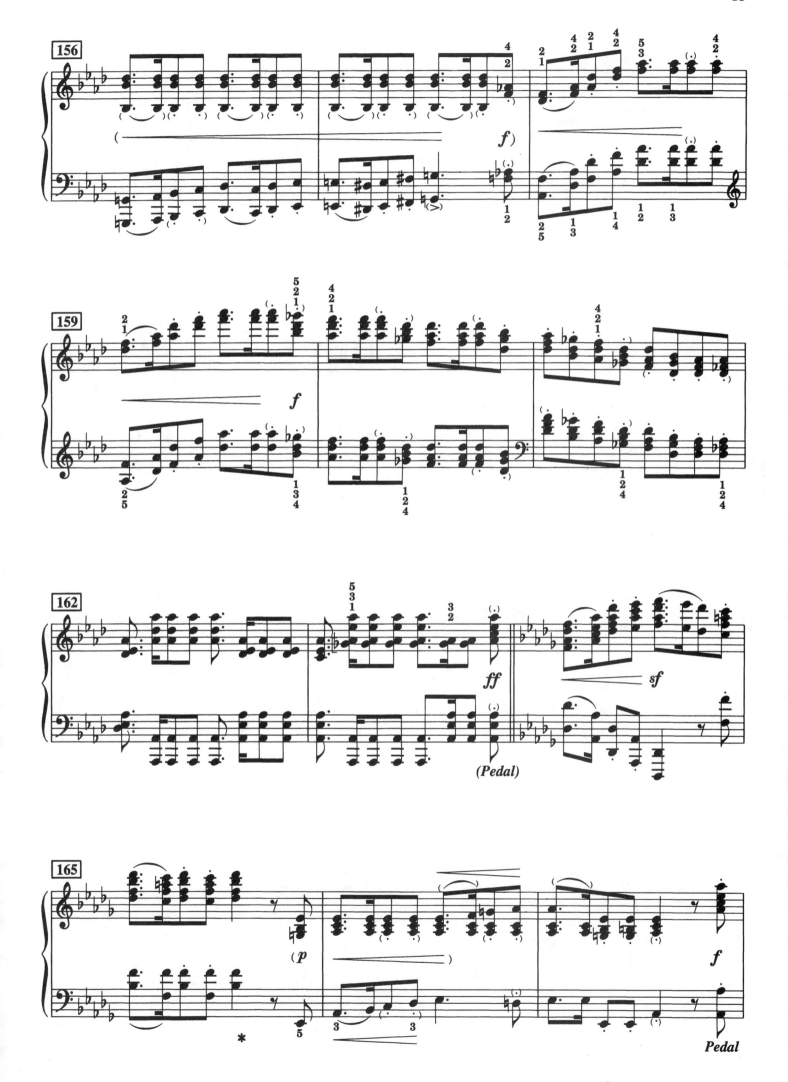

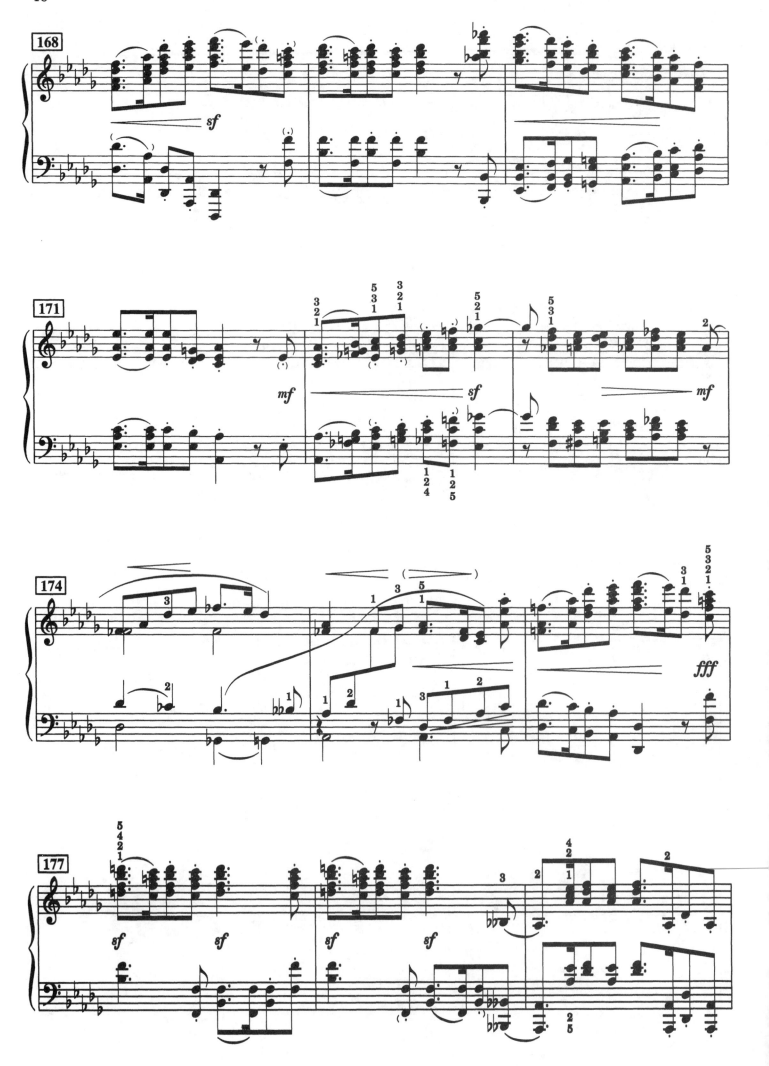

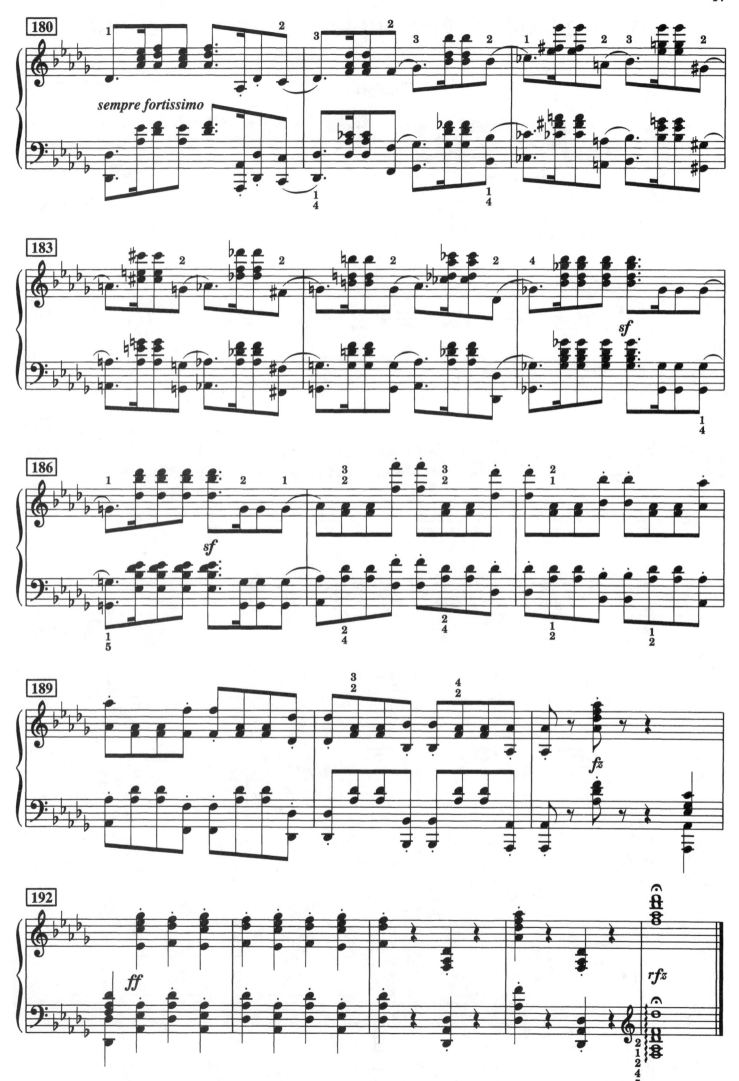

Appendix of Five Supplementary Variations[a]
to the *"Symphonic Etudes"*

Variation I

[a] Notes and signs in small print in these five variations (published posthumously) are contained in the autograph only.

49

Variation II

53

(a) The appoggiatura chords are dotted half notes without appoggiaturas in the autograph, which omits the octaves.

Variation III

Variation IV

Variation V ⓐ